For J, E and C.
Because I love you!

The book you have in your hands is a collection of our family's favourite sayers and prayers that we wrote over the years. Young children love rituals and repetitions. They provide familiarity and comfort in a life which is still so new. A life that holds so many exciting experiences and impressions every day.

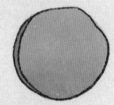

This is how this book came about! Our family found that starting our mealtimes and bedtimes with a short rhyme would ground our little ones. These poems helped our children focus and calm down, and ultimately became precious moments and memories. Of course, it made them incredibly proud that they knew all these rhymes by heart and we would leave it up to them to pick the ones they wanted to share.

Whilst most of the children's prayers I found in other books, were all fairly religious, I wanted my poems to focus on empathy, values and the awareness of how fortunate we are. Something tasty to eat, a warm and safe place to sleep, and the support and love of a family are privileges that not everyone gets to have.

For some of the mealtime poems we invented gestures to match the text. The rhyme, 'Lots of Little Fishes' for instance was accompanied with our hands put together, moving them like fish swimming about.

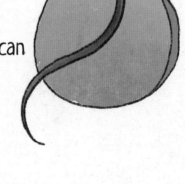

Encourage your children to make up their own gestures. It's wonderful to see how many surprising ideas they can come up with. And sometimes it's also perfect to just hold hands together and be close.

The rhymes are kept in the form we used them in, but you can easily tailor each and every one according to your personal family situation.

These poems brought us laughter, lots of happiness and bonding moments we will treasure forever. I really hope they do the same for your family!

JD Evers

SAYERS & PRAYERS

On my pillow I rest my head,

The day is done, it's time for bed.

Thank you for a lovely day,

And all your guidance on my way.

Please let my dreams be free from sorrow,

And grateful I will wake tomorrow.

For another day to come,

Filled with happiness, joy and fun.

I close my eyes and say good night,

Now Mummy please turn off the light.

Fluffy pillow, cosy cover,

Thank you for my mum, I love her.

Thank you for my daddy too,

He tickles me when I feel blue.

Thank you for my cuddly bed

And for the happy day I had.

All snuggled up now for the night,

I close my eyes and sleep real tight.

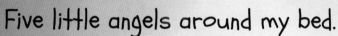

Five little angels around my bed.

One to my feet and one to my head.

One for my dreams and one to pray.

And one to shoo my fears away.

Please watch over me all night.

And wake me with the morning light.

Hurry little mousie,

Come out of your housey.

Go see what's been prepared for you,

Could be familiar or something new.

Not every meal can be your favourite,

Be grateful for the food and savour it.

Try everything... at least a bit,

Your taste buds might be loving it.

Holding hands, we lower our head,

Grateful for the lovely meal we'll get.

Remembering the ones who haven't enough,

Who are a living a life that is way more tough.

Praying for those without a home,

And also those who eat all alone.

We're very lucky and we know it,

By saying grace we want to show it.

Now's the time we start to eat.

Come on all, let's take a seat!

We're holding hands. We're being grateful,

For every glass and every plateful.

We're happy that we eat together,

In company all food tastes better.

It all started with 'Mousie, Mousie'. This was the first rhyme we put together when my son was only a few months old. It soon became our night-time favourite and I loved it, because it always made him chuckle when I tickled his hand at the end.

The intention of "Mousie, Mousie" is to bring the child to a point where he feels calm and at peace with himself. This is why it isn't just a rhyme, but it comes with a finger game to make it more engaging and fun.

Start circling your index finger around the outer line of your child's palm and begin with the rhyme. Keep circling, slowly making your way further inside the palm. And when you say the last line of the last verse, gently tickle your child's palm with all your fingers, signaling that Mousie's day is over and he can now go to sleep.

My little one still asks me to recite "Mousie, Mousie" for him now that he is already attending school. I guess, we both have so many fond memories that we might keep saying this one forever – just for the fun of it...

And if I'm lucky enough to be a grandmother one day, surely I'll be sharing the rhyme with these little ones too.

The rhyme works best with two-syllable names. If your child's name has more or less syllables, simply use a nickname or add a "ie/y" to the end of the name, such as Ann/Annie or Tim/Timmy.

Mousie, Mousie circle 'round.

Until [name of child] peace has found.

Mousie, Mousie circle deep.

Until [name of child] falls asleep.

Mousie please let [name of child]'s dream.

Be the best it's ever been.

Lots of little fishes,

Waiting for their dishes.

Swimming with their kin,

Holding each other's fin.

Everybody came,

Thinking all the same:

No matter what the food will be,

Enjoy your meal. Bon appétit!

When I am sad or things don't seem fair,

It can make me feel like you just don't care.

And when I ask, "Will you please help me out?",

But I can't have it my way,

I sometimes have doubts.

Yet deep inside I do understand,

That you must have had

Something different planned.

->

I know that you answer all prayers, although

Sometimes your answer will simply be no.

Please forgive me, when I doubt,

Don't understand you from the start.

If you hear me whine or pout,

Please just listen through my heart.

Monday when I fold my hands,
I ask you, bless my grandma. Thanks!

Tuesday then I hope and pray,
That you protect my mum.
Please keep her safe through every day,
Just like you've always done.

Wednesday's wish will never end:

I'll always hold my grandpa's hand.

->

Every Thursday,

My only request:

Please care for our daddy

'Cause he is the best!

Comes Friday I am asking you,
To look after my brothers too.

->

And for myself on Saturdays,

I pray in many different ways.

Please make me strong and just and good,

And help me live life as I should.

When Sunday finally comes my way,
For my whole family I pray.

Care for them all,
I love them so dearly.
And for listening all week,
God, I thank you sincerely!

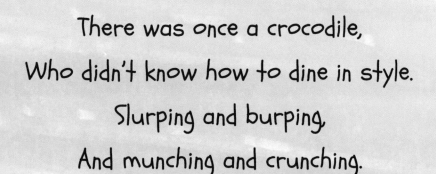

There was once a crocodile,

Who didn't know how to dine in style.

Slurping and burping,

And munching and crunching.

You could hear him all over,

While he was lunching.

It was his way to show,

That the food was so yummy.

And after the meal,

He rubbed his big tummy...

...and farted...wholehearted...

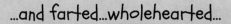

Write your very own poems and have fun colouring these pages!

First published in Great Britain and Germany in 2021 by JDE Publishing

ISBN paperback: 978-3-949053-00-9
ISBN ebook: 978-3-949053-01-6

Illustrations by Dajana Hoffmann
Text and illustrations copyright © JD Evers, 2021
All rights reserved

We're happy to receive your feedback and suggestions:
jdePublishing@gmail.com

Written by JD Evers
Illustrations by Dajana Hoffmann
Edited by Stephanie Stahl (stephaniestahl.com)

A CIP catalogue record for this title is available from the British Library and the German National Library.

Printed in Great Britain
by Amazon

10398011R10025